BECAUSE

LIFE

IS

WEIRD

AND

I

OVERTHINK

Jay Chirino

ISBN: 979-8-218-27066-7

To Liz
Because the world crumples without you

CONTENTS

ACKNOWLEDGMENTS

Writing good poetry, in my opinion, is about going through Life with eyes open and a heart that refuses to play it safe, to hide from the pain, the darkness, the misery that being human sometimes brings. It is welcoming the dimness of a rainy summer afternoon, and the tears that fall when the sudden silence of the monitoring equipment in a hospital room sinks deep in your bones, making you feel like bursting from within. In order to have those experiences (and write good poetry) you need others, people that will teach you things, that will give you priceless gifts, that will see you in ways you could never see yourself. In my case I have a few people to thank for that (the list of people that truly change your life is usually not long, and that is a good thing): my parents, my grandmother, my son, my wife. And those friends who ended up becoming family, you know who you are. Thank you for giving me the juice to write.

THE

DESTRUCTIVE

SELF

Poison

They don't understand that
this poison is the best medicine
because it lets me forget
because it pauses the cassette tape
that rewinds all these painful memories in my head
and plays them over and over again

They don't get the relief I get
from no longer feeling guilty
from no longer being scared
from no longer being me

And so I will continue to die
one swallow at a time

As Death is freedom, don't you see
Death is the release
from these chains, from this prison
that I keep putting myself
back in

Perhaps this poison
is really the medicine

Afraid

Afraid of dying, I
kill myself a little every day
so I can numb the panic
so I don't see when Death
decides to come
my way

The Good Stuff

11 am and the thirst begins to choke me
waves of saliva flooding
my tongue like a tsunami,
the dryness in my throat
drowning me in relentless desire
for the stuff…
the good stuff…

the only stuff that can truly quench
                              my pain

11 am and this day
has already overstayed its welcome,
has already made its presence
unfathomable, precocious
disgustingly
ordinary—the clock traveling to
the usual destinations;
the same minute of every
unpalatable hour, which cannot be dealt without
the stuff
the good stuff…

The stuff that I call medicine—although
there is a skull with crisscrossed
bones on the label—the stuff that
makes people more pleasant
to be around, but makes me
undesirable

The stuff that allows me to
forget that I hate everything in
this world,

 mostly myself

Crimson Vomit

Red wine stains are
hard to get off the carpet
in the apartment you share
with the wife that
will soon
end up leaving

Yet you
drink too much,
anyway
and you throw it up
anyway
and you couldn't make it
to the toilet
in time

And there you are
on your knees
scraping crimson vomit
off the beige rug
as she walks in
and gets a bit closer to
walking out the door
as you slowly rot

Eyes Of The Monster

Who is this being
that controls my
thoughts right now?
Is it the reckless madman
who wants to see
the world burn?
Is it the hopeful idiot
that is convinced
he can change?

Whose eyes are these
that I see through today?
Is it the one that thinks
there is no tomorrow?
Is it the one that pleads
for his life with
a monster?

The Meaning Of Everything

Nothing to say,
this universe is
meaningless
and all its
stars wasted

Daily Dose Of Hate

No wonder they think it's easy to
go through life smiling, ecstatic
jumping jacks and lots of laughter
it won't get better than this world,
elastic
full of possibilities,
flexible
for your convenience
for your appreciation
of what we do here
without remorse

No wonder they think it's easy
when they've never awoken
convinced that today
is the day to
pull the trigger
with mouth wide
open

After all, the sun
seems to be shining like
any other day
and the medication may work a little,
anyway

Everyone's "happiness"
is my daily dose of hate

One Day More

Alcohol is not used
by those with empty souls
it is consumed by the
overthinkers of the world
the ones that can't keep
the engine from overheating
the ones whose thoughts
run like wild stallions through the clearing
the ones that see something dull
in the in the everydayness
the ones that know that
these worlds will not recuperate
the ones that see Death coming
like a demonic train with no brakes
the ones that understand the true
value of the human chase
the ones that lost everything
because everything was not enough
the ones that the world rejected
even before they were born

These people don't drink for pleasure,
they drink to be able to withstand
one day more

Manufactured Peace Of Mind

I am obsessed with
peace of mind of
the chemical type;
anxiety doesn't care for
positive thinking
or meditative states
or Kundalini sweats
there is no time to waste
in hypnotic regression
or fervent prayers to
invisible gods

I simply cannot
do it alone
I do not trust
myself that much
I need blooming mycelium spores
and cannabis paranoia
and instant neuron intoxication to
blur the expectations of
imminent non-existence

I need reality to be
fuzzy, dream-like
its sharp edges dulled
its long suffering muted
maybe not all the way down
but just enough

I have swelling of the mind
I have misery of the heart
I have disenchantment of the spirit
I have no time to fix what was born broken, so

Chemically indulge me
if only temporarily; gift me
manufactured peace of mind

Warrior

On those days that
the sun rises
without you
the bed becomes
a guardian angel
washing your face
feels like being
waterboarded and
your pajamas become
your armor…

On those days that
alcohol becomes
medicine and
medicine becomes
cancer,
those are the days
you shall become
a warrior;
as even at your lowest
you will refuse
to stop fighting

Rust Bucket

It's sad really
the sabotage I have inflicted
upon this perfectly good body
the holes I have drilled in its frame
the worn out breaks I have
yet to change
the bald tires that are
running out of air

I am terrified of accidents,
yet always seem to be
setting myself up for one
and when I muster the courage
to call a mechanic,
I hang up the phone before they can
reply

It's sad, really
knowing I could've had it all
I could've gone anywhere in
this great big world
but this body that I inhabit
is now a rust bucket that
will soon find its dwelling
by the side of
a dying sun

A Good Day

It's a shitty day
when the failures return
and insecurities you thought
long ago forgotten
once again
knock at the door
holding a bottle of wine
and wearing a party hat

"Hey! Let's celebrate big boy!
It's been a while!
Let's get drunk and talk
about how you
aren't what you
think you are."

"It sounds enticing,"
you say. "But things are
not what they used to be
the wine is no longer appealing
and I have to work in the morning."

It's a shitty day
when the assholes at work
make you miserable
when the assholes in traffic
make you angry
when humanity itself
becomes a
self-destructive virus

But hey,
at least you didn't drink
and that
makes today
a good day.

Broken Man

The broken man is
broken not because he
does not know how to
fix himself
but because he cannot
avoid
consistently destroying
what he has already
built

Finish Line

You are at peace now
the demons who tortured
the child inside
no longer able to use your
withering body for their
selfish appetites

The chase is over
you can stop running now

The cigarette smoke
no longer has to paint
the ceiling of your apartment
on the sleepless nights
filled with rum

The liquor can now cease
to pretend it was a friend
that it was protecting you
from something
erasing bad memories
letting you forget
leaving you with nothing
but regret and the sting
of a wasp on your tongue

You did it
you killed the monster within
even if you had to go along

The chase is now over
you can let go

16

THE

CRITIC

Contradiction

I'm a quiet soul
but I talk too much
I'm a wandering spirit
but I sleep past noon
I'm a true romantic
but refuse to love
I honor sobriety
but I drink too much
I enjoy the words
but don't write them all
I'm a family man
but like being alone
I'm not afraid of death
but refuse to go
I'm a contradiction
born between two words

Oil And Water

How many times
must I learn the same lesson:
they simply cannot handle
the entire you
the euphoric you
the secret you who
becomes free when he
feels safe, when he feels
there is nothing better than
to be himself

And then come the reminders
the annoyances
the complaints about how
you talk too much
you laugh too loud
"Go back to the silent version
of this clown, get back to
miming, won't you?
Until we ask you to speak"

How many times will I have to
be reminded that people and I
are like water and oil
they can dwell together in
the same container

Yet they will never mix

Terminal Velocity

Sometimes this feeling of disappointment
reaches terminal velocity
like the parachute that won't open
like the man who drinks too much

I hoped that growing up would
change things,
but nothing feels
more like a dream than
looking for the best in people

I am ashamed to be called of your kind
it disturbs me to know
that the blood running through
your veins is the same shade of red as mine

The worthlessness of your actions,
of your selfishness,
of your escalating hubris,
badly reflects on the god
that took credit for making you

Sometimes I wish I was never born
if it also stifled
the birth of you

Free Will?

What does it mean
to be free?

Do I have some agency
over the outpour
of ideas that
constantly flow
through me?

Can I manage to
go to war with
nature, and win?

Is the environment
stronger than
my father, or
is the blood in
my veins what
dictates who
I am?

Should I even
strive for change
or is this world
a fantasy being
projected against
the canvass of
the mind?

Little Factory

There is a factory in my head
manufacturing excuses, and
even though it has high quotas
it strives to meet them every day

Production started years ago and
there has never been a shutdown
as Treasurer and CEO, I am
usually impressed by its output

There is never a lack of material
from which to fabricate from
we produce any excuse required
to be able to say "no"

And this little factory seems
to never be slowing down
it will continue production until
I am deep underground

My Mind's Mind

My mind seems to have
a mind of its own, it keeps
its own secret thoughts, and deliberately
attempts to sabotage my soul

I am not sure why, but I have
a strong suspicion that my mind
hates me

My mind seems to have a
latent desire to see the world burn
to send everything and everyone
to hell
to get drunk and erase itself
to get high and blame me
for the mistakes it made
when I was not awake

Perhaps I should
let it do what it wants to
so I can bargain
to have time to rest

Fortified

Yesterday I was going
to rule the world
confident no one
could stop me
even if they tried

Today these bed sheets
have manufactured
the perfect warmth,
immobilizing my body
expunging every desire
for victory I ever had

They say the enemy
awaits on the other side
of fortified walls
I'm not really sure if
that is true, but just in case it is
I'm going to sleep in a little more

Biggest Enemy

The enemy
who terrifies me most
is the one that seeks to
destroy my plans
never allowing me to
reach my goals
It's the one that
constantly berates and
drills holes of doubt
in my already
weakened confidence;
the one that chortles
when I strategize and
softly whispers in my ear:
"you will never get to be
the person you wish to be
you will never get to go
to places you've never been
you will never get the love
of which you have always dreamed"

The enemy I am most terrified of
is the enemy that
dwells within

Drowning

And I continue to sink
as the doubt pulls me deeper
towards the bottom of the abyss

Is this who I am
really supposed to be, or is the illusion
projecting onto canvass of my soul
attempting to
deceive me?

Velcro

Sticky like Velcro, my mind
sticks to the things
that make it panic
like a hoarder of scary movies
like the madness of
seeking fear as if
it was a gift

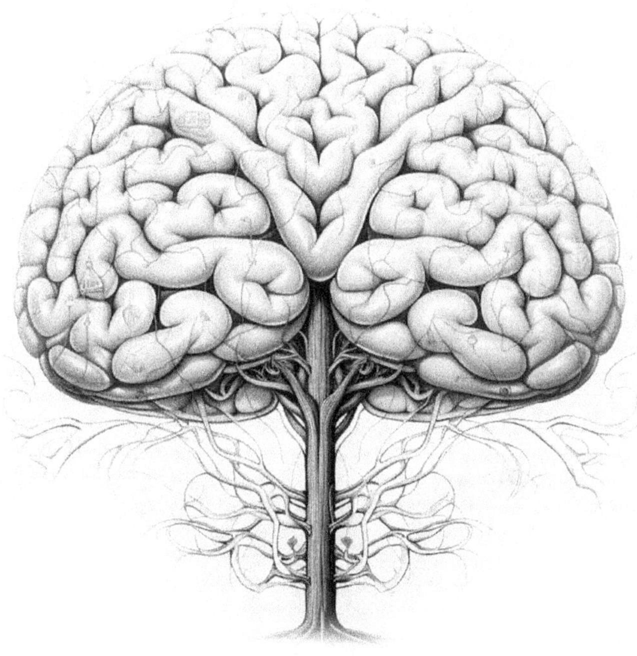

Demon

I want to
undress the ocean and
bathe in the blood
of Time

I want to
escape the nightmares
that dwell under the bed
of my mind

I want to
break free from
the chains of my master;
the demon within that
pursues one last
drink

But the master is
the scared child that
I used to be
the demon is that
little kid who just
wants to run free

How do I vanish the demon
when the demon is
a part of me?

Forgiveness Not Allowed

The past calls
through my dreams
and I beg, please!
Don't let me see
a child born of
innocence
through suffering
discovering what
the world truly is

Yet the mind
remembers and
it won't forgive
as those old days
shaped it to what
it came to be
and when I feel
happy, careless and
free
it sends stern reminders
at night,
through my dreams

The broken child inside
won't allow me to forget
won't allow me to forgive

Professional Victim

Take me away from
this hell that I
have proudly created
for myself

I chase the demons away
only to invite them
again

Why do I feel useless
if I don't play
the victim?

Forecast

I am empty
yearning for cold water
from a wasted barrel
with a thousand holes

I am crazy
thinking I would
find fulfillment
in an empty world

Nothing feels
refreshing going
down my throat
Hope is a field of roses
that will never grow

I am steady
firm in my conviction
like never before;
this world is
meant for darkness

With it we shall
fall

Feline Observations

My cat has observations
about the clothes I often wear
Sometimes she really hates it when
I wear the same pajamas every day
I think she can smell the stink
of depression on them, the defeat
of lost struggle, the silence of
a mind that weeps

Perhaps she knows that now she
must meow a little harder
lightly stomp on my chest with her paws
maybe a careful bite on my hand
just to get me to fall awake and
struggle on my feet to feed her

She doesn't mind it, though

She will lay at the end of the bed
curled under the warmth of sheets
that haven't been changed
surrounded by the darkness of windows
that stay shut, in a room filled with
dust and sadness

She doesn't mind, she knows it's all temporary
she knows the closet is filled with
fresh shirts, and pants and underwear
and all she has to do is wait there, patiently
until the room comes alive again

Lazy Mattress

And they call you lazy because
you have chosen to keep
the drapes closed and the
door locked, a cool
darkness misting the room
you sleep in

And your side of the bed
has certain indentations
you have made with
time and gravity alone, the weight of
your planked body exerting
passive force on the mattress
carving hills and valleys made
out of foam and fabrics,
something you like to call:

A creation of my own

Even homeostasis can manufacture
new and unexpected shapes, which
in your darkness you can't help
but feel a little proud of
as it is validity of your presence
proof of your existence
your breathing body still strong enough
to make an impact on something

Something

No matter how insignificant

They call you lazy because
you don't see the purpose in
striving towards goals that will
one day be worthless
History the owner of the greatest
eraser, soon scrubbing everything
you once considered of value

Instead, you enjoy the glory of
leaving your shadow chiseled on the mattress
and that satisfies you enough to
want to live one more day

Cave

There is no better feeling
than canceling whatever
engagement you had at six
staying in your pajamas
and watching tv while
the world outside burns
yet, you are warm and cozy
and totally unbothered
about what drives people
crazy out there

Morning Conversations

"You look a little off today,"
they say
"a bit more tired than usual,
almost as if you woke up on
the shitty side of the bed"

Little do they know that
getting up from that bed
was nothing
short of a miracle,
comparable
to walking on water
or bringing a man back from death

Little do they know
about the argument I had
in order to convince
my mind it wasn't
the right day to die,
the perfect day to give up
the ideal morning to throw
it all out the window and
stay in bed a little more

Little do they know that
I feel triumphant about
simply being here, the darkness
I constantly wrestle being
once again defeated, and if
I look a little off or
a bit more tired than usual
that's ok with me,
at least I am here to be it

Shadow Banned

I think I may have been
shadow banned by Life's algorithm
barred to the same level
regardless of dedication
effort, planning, grit,
and hours of meditation

Perhaps I got busted by the Karma police
for prior indiscretions
for certain things I did
perhaps they have some shady data
stored on some server hidden
in a murky corner of
the digital plane

Maybe I was reported by
the girl who said she had been
treated unfair, by the friend
who said I hadn't been there
by my parents for the adolescent
escapes, by those that
witnessed my declining mental state,
back then, when I was lost in a web
of lies, false hopes, self-generated chaos
paranoid searches for illnesses that
I didn't have, job applications I lied on,
bosses I walked out on,
people whose expectations I couldn't
live up to, those that had seen me
without the mask

And now the data has been corrupted;
the light not enough to cover the darkness
I have forgotten the password for access
to the things that bring me joy
to the goals I want to reach
to the avatar I want to be
to the security word
for forgiveness

I have been cast out by a past
I can no longer change,
face up to the sky, eyes rotting in the sun
cloudless days destroying what it means to be me

I guess I must reboot and
start over again

Happiness, My Responsibility

And at the end of the day
no one should want it
more than you,
the sacrifice demanded to
fill an empty soul must
be made by the one who
carries the weight of
not being whole

The Angle Of Before

The night only has a certain shimmer
when you see it at the right angles,
when you twist your neck just enough
for your vision to absorb
the curious lucidity that one finds
in darkness

I have been broken for a while now
no one seems to notice, they
have seen me in pieces before
and this doesn't look like "before" to them

I think it is the fact that I have
been able to put a plausible costume
on "before" and paint its lips a
shady red, and go walking
down the street as a care-free
man would, a smile drawn with a pen
somewhat like before, now just a bit…
different

And they so desire for before never to
come back, oh no, never do come back
they take these structural mishaps as slight misunderstandings
because, before, before will
never be coming back. Oh no, never!
But I know…

That this anger sits upon me like a mad giant
squeezing the air from my lungs
and the hope from my heart, along with
my desires,

Because I know…
that the night only has a certain shimmer
when you see it at the right angles…

Home

I was birthed by this universe in 1983
it gave me a mother with protective spirit
a father who was a dreamer,
a womb to call my own and
a school to get me ready for
all that was to come

It taught me heartbreak at fifteen
It gave me wine at seventeen
It gave me hope at twenty-one and
It took it away a little later

It showed me deception coming from the strangest places
it gave me reasons for surrendering
and many more for becoming strong
it showed me that struggle brings growth
and that loneliness is to be treasured

This is my playground
this is my school
this is my battle
this is my home

This is the one and only perspective that
I am proud to call my own
and when the path turns to ruble
when there are no more lessons to be learned
when the birds fly through the beams of
a dying sun and the loved ones that were
are simply no more;
when the light dims to black and the colors disappear
I will take it all with me,
I will leave nothing behind
I will go where I belong

Old Buick

I had seen them
take off and land
a thousand times;
the airplanes would bring
and take people to new territories;
places where anything
was possible

My dad would drive some of them
to and from the airport
as I sat in the back seat
of his blue '49 Buick,
the one with the
Nova transmission and
the leaky fuel tank

The automatic doors
at the gate would open and
people walked in and out
of what felt like
another dimension
I stood there
hand holding my father's
wondering what it
was like to fly high in the sky
to go somewhere without
restrictions on how many
toys I could buy
or how much food was assigned

The years passed and
our turn finally came
we went through those doors
and we sat on that plane
"Do you like it?" Mom asked
as the turboprop rushed
down the runway
until it went fast enough
to get picked up by the air

I smiled as we climbed
and for the first time
the clouds were cushioned
under my feet
and through all the excitement
of these things coming true
a small twinge of sadness
put a tear in my eye,
for an instant realizing I
would never again sit in the back of
that old Buick
and dream

The Chase

He walked very fast
everywhere he went,
as if in an endless hurry
or simply just running late
my legs were short, but it didn't matter
I chased
almost running to keep up
"Dad, wait! Where are you going?"
"I have a TV to repair"
"Can I come and see you work?"
I would eagerly ask
"Sure," he'd smile and say
"just don't ask anything of strangers"
"The clients?"
"Yes, the strangers,
there is food when we get home."

And I would trot on the sidewalk
as he held me by a hand and
I tried keeping up with his
bigger than life steps
his toolbox bouncing
against his other leg
sweat running down our faces
in an unforgiving summer
and the customers offered water
that tasted as crisp as blades
and I sat next to him quietly as
he soldered away
a diode here, a capacitor there
"Why did you choose this job, dad?"
"Because I love movies and shows," he said
"Me too!"
and I still do
all these years later
he doesn't walk that fast anymore
but I still chase
to keep up

Mother

It was when all
hope had left me
and I was ready to
embrace the heat of
hellfire

That you looked in
my eyes with that
conviction that only
you have
and said:

"I know that
like a phoenix
you will rise again,
flying higher than ever
before, and making me
proud, most of all"

And right you were

They all remember
the year you gave me the gift of Life

I, instead, remember
the day you birthed me
for a second time

Remembrance

All the lessons learned
through years of immaculate tortures
all those lessons learned
vanish as if
the heat of the bottle
turns them into
vapor
and I become childlike again;
innocent, unknowing
eager to discover new and
strange territory
and yet, I have been there
time and time
again

My mind is not
concerned with
lessons, it does not
regard the outcomes of
the day as worthy of
remembrance,
it cares about
killing the pain
however the hell
it can

Breathe

Why can't I breathe? Why can't I spell the name of
my father as if I forgot it long ago?
Why do I feel that my essence
will take me where I don't belong?

Why does it feel like people
avoid looking in my eyes?
Why does it feel like the heavens
are not much brighter than the sky?

We want heroes to save us from darkness
their superpowers removing
responsibility from our shoulders
we want to become victims
we want to become vigilantes of truth
we want you to relish our weakness
and let us ponder at the sky

The Child Hides

The child hides from
what he fears most
from the unknown of
what has yet to be
experienced

I hide from telling
my father I love him

I hide from my own
potential

I hide from success
not achieved

I hide from lessons not
learned

I hide from losing
a friend

I hide from what love truly is

I hide from reaching
the end

But the child cannot
hide forever

And it will be Death
that will ultimately find him

Hearse

Someday I
will be the one
being taken for
a ride

Says the driver
of the hearse

Residue Of Me

Is this how it feels to
lose my mind,
through scrambled dreams
and tangled
memories that never
happened?

In the illusion of
failures hidden in
matters of things
that don't belong?

How does one know
what is real
when the mind chooses
its own despair?

Can one truly see in
the distance
how this narrative
will end?

I start to wonder if
I died years ago and all this
is just some
residue of
me that is
left

Every Day

Every day I
get a little closer to
my permanent place
of dwelling
where the walls are
made of earth and
only the earthworms
visit

Every day takes
a little bit of
my essence
dissolving in the stew of time,
inviting me into
the halls of
the forgotten
turning me invisible
one wrinkle at
a time

Every day I
fade away and
I am still not sure
that I have made a
difference

Will my life
end up having a
single speck of
significance?

Only when I am gone
will I know if I
existed

People, Places, Things

Little by little Life
keeps flipping the pencil
erasing vital parts of
my childhood
places, things,
people that mattered
because of interactions that
seemed insignificant to them
but somehow shaped me
to what I am today

Now they are gone and
I question myself
Do I really know me?
Did I truly know them?

People, places, things
now created by me
as they no longer exist
in the long-gone worlds out there

The Illusion Of Time

The needle follows its faithful journey
around the perimeter of time, keeping me in
this inescapable prison, in this system of lies

Some days seem to repeat themselves
carbon copies of each other, the needle
keeps ticking away, keeps ticking away
and I get lost in the forest of the mundane
of the everyday that I call my prison
of every minute of my own hell

One earns with time what one cannot with money
one wastes the time we're given on this earth
and if it's true it's all just an illusion
Life is a dream from which we shall awake

Gray Hairs

There are a
few more
gray hairs reflected
in the bathroom mirror;
a small reminder
that important
things have been
learned

Twenty years ago
my head was
the color of
a starless night
empty and
inexperienced;
a vessel
unaware of
what it was
made to
hold

Today I look
in the mirror and
there is a new
gray hair
striving to
stand out,
it's another
badge of honor;
the prize awarded
for being a
survivor

Fear Of The Future

Yes, you will be gone one day
I know that too well
and what will be left
if not the memory
of when the world was once complete

And the vast emptiness will
engulf me like a giant and
take me through the nightmare
of what it means to lose everything

Yes, I will always have the memories
but the memories won't be enough
what if I want to hug you
because I know that I never
hugged you enough?

What if the message on the cell phone
is not enough to hear your voice?

What if looking at your picture
doesn't fulfill me of the presence
of your soul?

What if I need you to drive me to
that place where we would go
and it was the actual drive together
what we both were going for?

What if I just need to cry and
have YOUR shoulder to lean on?

Yes, you will be gone one day
but you shall not go alone,
the deepest part of me
with you shall fly away
as this world without you
will not have a reason
or a purpose
anymore

Eyes

You saw me
open these eyes for the first time
these eyes have seen so much
but were so innocent back then, so
hopeful…
that the world would be what it isn't, yet
and you tried to shield me
from what you knew this was;
this, this thing we call Life
this thing we suffer through.

Then you promised
you would be here forever
to always protect me
from the inevitable
now, you sit there, blind
those eyes have seen so much
too much, like mine
and more

And I lift you off that wheelchair, and promise
I will be here forever
to shield you from this thing…
this thing we call Life
but you've been there already
and you already know
that there are things that don't last long
and long has been already
and soon you will be gone

And I will be here to shield you
from what you already know
at least for a little while
until you eyes go quiet
as they have seen so much,
yet I know that
fantasies are just that,
fantasies

As one never sees too much
one never lives too much
one never loves too much
one never hopes enough
when your eyes saw this world
for the first time
and will see it once more
for the last
I will be there to protect you
from what the world has never been
and you will become a memory
impatient, distilled
one of the most important
and necessary things
my eyes have ever seen,
in your end, I will protect you
as this thing we call Life
reminds us of that day
we grieved

THE

WRITER

Old Friends

Back in the day
when there wasn't
anything to chase
the fear away or
to numb the pain
just a little
all I had was
the paper and
the pen
to work out the feelings

Hello, old friends
you have remained
loyal through the years
and I will do the same

Wings Made Of Words

I found these wings
made of words and I
put them on for the
sake of trying

I ran towards the
cliff without any
expectation, death
no longer a fear but
a desired anticipation

But these wings caught
the breeze and cradled
me toward the heavens
and I flew higher
than those beings who
like to call themselves
angels

The bird is in the air
and I am not sure
where it is headed
but I know it won't
stop flying until
we know that we
got there

Hunter Of Thoughts

These words that sometimes
come and sometimes do not

The relentless exercise
required to produce a
decent thought while
swimming in a pool filled
with mediocrity…

(and they worship it)

Sometimes I drown
sometimes I fly
sometimes the emptiness
fills the mind like
the color blue fills the sky

Sometimes I wonder why
I do it at all

Why do I stand on the
tracks of a rushing train
that carries the dreadful
truths of the world

Just to collide with a thought
worthy of eternal life
on the page?

These Words

Because all I have are these words
this is my weapon, given by God
this is my only protection
against the ones attacking with ignorance
the ones that fight without rules
the ones whose hatred is merciless
whose joy is whatever they can extract
from others

All I have are these words

Sometimes filled with doubt and
others filled with wonder
often used as a breastplate to
cover my heart under
others used as a poem to
remind them how much
I love them

All I have are these words and
they seem so feeble, so forgetful
they jump from thought to thought
like butterflies seeking nectar
and often I don't remember what
I wanted to used them for
and the years I've collected
wish not to help me anymore

All I have are these words

The only thing my grave will host
besides my rotting body
the wafting memory of a poet
the dying scent of a rose;
like a bed of feathers I hope these
words shall choose to carry me
intolerably, determined
to eternity and beyond

Waiting For The Flow

Sometimes the words
flow like water
down the river
today the river
has dried out
the current does not
want to flow through
the sulci of the mind
and it becomes static;
paralyzed, lost in a
sea of thoughts that
it's unable to
describe

"Don't try"
Said Bukowski

I shall sit here
And wait for
the fly

Fissure

This, right here is
the fissure where the doubt
seeps through, here on the ceiling,
right above the lightbulb that shines
on my desire to succeed,
on the yearning for being more
than what the manual stated I
was designed to be

Tiny drops steadily, rhythmically
fall through this hole
—like Chinese water torture—
each drop more excruciating than
the last, intolerable pain
that rains on visions of the past
making microscopic dents inside
my confidence, rusting the
metal scaffolding that holds up
the determination to keep on

At first you think nothing of it
how much damage can a little
water do?

It is the unwavering persistence
of the process through time
which makes a crater
from a pinhole

Writer's Block

Nothing worth writing
is coming out at
this time, I don't know if
my mind is fried, or I am simply
terrified of all this being
just a glimmer of unfounded hope

Lightning strikes a time
or two on the paper, but can
it be quantified?
Can it be duplicated?

Sometimes I think
the last poem will be the last
and I will not be able
to survive without putting
a word down, somewhere
but what if the word is not
a word but a pretentious
statement of what I think
Life is without even knowing
how to describe what
surrounds me anymore; this
pain of knowing that I
exist for nothing more than
the entertainment of the gods,
but the gods themselves do
not exist and I am just here:
a speck of dust in an
improbable world that will
explode one day and not
even the shadow of the things
I said and
wanted to say
will remain

Eternal Life

I want to
die without regrets
without unanswered
questions

I want to lay on
the bed of flowers
that opens heaven's
doors, without
wondering "what if"
I would have done
a little more

Life is fragile and
Death is complete
an eternity of
regrets is not
what I desire
left of me

Every word
I type on this
keyboard, I want it
to outlive me,
a thousand years
from now
only through them
I'll be breathing

THE

ROMANTIC

The Choice

Let me down
bring me peace
Allow me to stop trying

Let me die
let me live
just don't leave me hanging

It's the uncertainty that
feels like death
validation of my worthlessness
in your presence

Is it truth, is it lies?
I choose either to the game
that you play with
twisted eyes

Bring me love
give me peace

I'll take loneliness
instead

Demented

I woke up one morning and
couldn't recognize you,
you were a silhouette
standing by the door
surrounded by a whitish glow
that made its way towards the bed

You walked in
wearing a sad little smile
your lips kissed my forehead
a random tear left your eye

And then that sweet glow
engulfed you and
you disappeared, forever

Sometimes
I forget you once
loved me

Sometimes
I regret that you
existed at all

Sometimes
I wish these memories
would carry me to sea
and drown me
once and for all

Upside Down

This is what you always do
light the gas to the light
overshadow the truth, you
come out from behind the curtain
with this act that you do
victimizing every decision I
have made for my truth

This is what you always do
manufacture guilt and give it as
a gift; sleepless nights
filled with heartache and doubt
about the paradigm of my reality

I no longer know myself
I don't know the difference
between the truth and
what you say

This is what you always do
you take my sanity in the
palm of your hand, wrapping
your fingers around it and
squeezing as if
suffocating a baby bird

And I feel like I'm drowning
falling, flying, the sky upside down
the trees rooted from the clouds
I am trying to claw out of this
nightmare,

But you won't let me touch the ground

You Win

I know it was never
you intention to hurt me
your selfish ways were
known to everyone but you,
you didn't know that the love
you were supposed to give me
had been attached to the
kite string of your truth

And now, of course,
you have become the victim
my wounds have healed and
no evidence remains
of countless times when
on my knees I begged you
to please forgive me and
rather choose to stay

Little did I know that
long before that day
you had already made your decision
and wrote it with indelible ink
then just waited for
the argument forecasted
to make your exit and
forever go away

I gave it on a silver platter, exactly as
you had expected, while
tearing a piece of my soul
just to understand your justice;
to comprehend how soon
one can forget it all

I know it was never your
intention to hurt me,
but hey, what was said
was said, and what is done
is done, and if your role was
to decisively play the victim

you certainly got the job
well done

Victims

We were victims, you and I, of
circumstantial altercations that
swept our bodies and minds
rendering us useless in certain situations
ignorant of the things that mattered;
a blurry image through the lenses
of stigmas and lies

See, we were set for failure, you and I
unrealistic expectations and societal dilemmas
impregnated our very souls with
borrowed views and opinions that blinded us
that chained us to eternal darkness
we were both thrown inside a garden
where love could never grow and
asked to thrive under such circumstances

And then the veil was lifted and
you saw who I really was: A stranger
one that was broken and sad
that wasn't truly aware of his surroundings
that didn't know how to act
and you, with your vane expectations and
selfish arguments, with your imported desires
of how they told you things should be
you couldn't handle the rawness of a reality
that was always hidden

The flimsy thought of staying and fighting
quickly flew out of you
like a butterfly ready to go on a quest
to entice the next flower

Yet I don't blame you,
we were victims
you and I
of something bigger
something darker

Somehow we survived
we drew our own lines, carved our own paths
maybe not as perfect or pure
but truly ours for the first time
the most real representation of
who we truly are; the true iteration
of our limited freedoms
because at the end of everything

we were slaves and nothing more

Feeling Good

Let me
sit here and
enjoy this pain.
It feels so good
as it means I
loved you

Melted Gold

You found me broken and
for some reason you
decided to put me back together again
like the shattered
Japanese pot that
becomes more beautiful
by sealing its cracks
with melted gold

Loving you is simple
yet exhilarating
filling every atom of
my being, programming my
DNA to let me love carelessly
strengthening my bones
to go to war, like a warrior, if necessary

Then you go and
take me through time
like a traveler of galaxies
like a jumper of universes
every quantum version of
me helplessly in love with
you, in every dimension

You are simply and
unequivocally
my new reality, and I
the ultimate paradigm of
a new person
constructed with
discarded scraps
and for that I love you
more than I ever have

Assault

You fulfilled me
as if the universe had
never allowed me to
take a full breath before
when your lips interfered with
my gasp at your willingness
for a kiss

And you oxygenated my lungs
filled my heart with love
in a way the best doctors
had not been able to before,
their diagnosis never
found a true solution
for the dying soul

And so I owe my life to you
and your patient forever I'll be
as there is nothing more that
fills my heart like an assault
from your lips

Lifesaver

I want to talk until
my windpipe is rotten, my flesh
unceremoniously returned to
the ground

I want to laugh until
my laughter is the only thing left
in existence, atoms dissipating
through the black hole of Mind…
is suffering the only deal that seems ideal;
solely through the lenses of the past?

Is happiness the illusion of having
a path to experiencing such circumstance;
a love circumstance, a hope circumstance, a
redemptive absorption of the essence that
makes ME what I am NOT?

Yes! I want to laugh until
my smile is plastered and permanent, unpersuasive, like concrete…
Oh baby, save me from something!
Oh baby, save me from me!

Shadow

Let them argue about
who rules the world or
who has truly
seen God

Let them spend
entire lives trying
to figure out what
it's all about

You and I have known it
for a little while now:

As long as we are
together all else
becomes a shadow

Alive

Put the top down
let's go for a ride
let us have an
adventure in this
thing we call
Life

What a thrill to
see you smile

We are alive
you and I
let's have this
moment forever
this moment
will never
die

Enough

Something tells me
this planet was not
designed for the
likes of us
you and I, dreamers
that should have been
born in a different time,
a different world

The ones we live amongst
have become addicted
to chaos, lovers of
the self-imposed narrative,
junkies who lust for
one another, for orgasms
that arrive too quick
diggers of craters deep
in their hearts, which
they are unable to fill

And yet, you and I
do not seem eager to
join such movements
that seek self-awarded
reputations and manufactured
stories, filtered through lenses of
lives that no one is living

You and I just want
what we want:
we want to live
we want to love
we want to cry
we want to die

and that will be enough

Warm Blankets

Oh, but you see love
it's not that I am lazy
when I refuse to
rise with the sun
it's just that
the heat of your body
under the blankets
soothes my soul
exfoliates my skin
keeps my cold heart warm
and makes me want to live
under these sheets
forever

Why should I go wrestle
this rabid bear of a world
when your body provides
all the necessities?

Amongst The Stars

Morning always arrives
no matter how much
I beg it not to
because at night this bed
holds everything that
soothes my heart:
the cat, the dog,
you… my copilot as
we travel through the stars
in this spaceship made of
bedsprings and blankets
and pillows

And we wrap around each other
as the room disappears and
the dreams that come
seem so trivial
when I have paradise here
right by my side
in a king sized piece of heaven
real estate of the divine
where love has erected walls
to keep the rest of the world
outside,
our snores the little engine
that soon is going to make us fly
farther than ever
we have a full
fuel tank
inside a beating heart

But morning still arrives
our spaceship lands and
we must now kiss goodbye
if only for a little while;
the cat must get fed
the dog must get walked
the bills must get paid

Yet, as morning arrives
at just the right time
so does the night
and our little spaceship
will be fueled, ready
for another trip
amongst the stars

Dreams Of You

Even after all this
time, being with you
feels like skating
through the substrate
of a dream

There is something here
not truly rooted in
the foundation of
the real

I stay terrified of
suddenly awaking
it would be like
dying in a thousand lives
and losing the very glue
that holds the Universe
together

88

THE

WATCHER

The World Hurts

The world hurts
like the sting of
an angry wasp
like the wound from
a hateful lie
like the bite of
a rabid word

The world hurts
and sometimes
the pain is excruciating
a thousand needle pricks
piercing your faith
in the truth of a humanity
you no longer find
meaningful

The world hurts
but you continue to
push forward past
the thorny curtains of
deception; closer
to discovering what lies
on the other side of
the mirage

And yet,
sometimes illusions are often
better off left
intact

Hurt

Why hurt to hurt
to never give up
to be finally erased and
to be demoted to dust?

Why love to love
to find fulfillment in love
to finally grieve and
leave it behind in a song?

Why breathe just to breathe
just to pretend that living
is better than laying beneath?
Simply because your chest rises
with every breath and
deflates with your exhale
does not mean that your
value exceeds the ones
who already took all breaths
and did everything their
time allotted

And here you are,
feeling superior
as you think you understand
the value you have
to give, when there is
no more value in hubris,
there is no more value
in sin

The Most Unfortunate Animal

The most unfortunate animal

is the one conscious of his own existence
and the futility of it

is the one aware of time
and its diminishing brevity

is the one aware of death
and its imminent arrival

is the one aware of love
knowing it won't last forever

is the one aware of light
because he has whirled in darkness

The most unfortunate animal

is the one that knows he holds little value
in an unforgiving world

Divine

Fragile like a vase,
the body;

It shatters with old age,
the mind;

A shortened sense of time,
experience;

You are temporary
but divine

Majestic

Oh, how the body withers
like the flower that's been ripped
from the sun
like the leaves that
rustle and fall and depart
once they're detached from the source
and they crumble and break
the wind sweeping them away
never to be seen again
never to be part of something called
Majestic

Handful Of Flames

"Out of all the days you
get to breathe air"—
said the old man—
"most are insubstantial;
forgettable
while many others
hurt like hell

Then there are
a few here and
there (he smiles
a toothless grin)
a handful in
a lifetime that
save you from
the flames"

Dust Specks

You get older and almost suddenly
people around you begin to die
aunts, uncles, grandparents you loved
because they were present in some of
your best childhood memories,
and others you never quite saw much
but they seemed to constantly be there
through the years of your growth

Not anymore

And every death is like erasing
a color from the wheel, making
Life a little bit duller, a little bit grayer
it's like plucking a petal off the flower
the awareness that it has not many left
letting you know that your day
is getting closer, the day when you
will be the discarded color, the petal
ripped away and left to crumple in
the morning sun

By then the rainbow will be gone and
the flower will have withered
and perhaps, you will be ok with that;
anxious, expectant of what comes next
greatly hoping that somehow you will
end up in the same place that they
all went

Maybe you also will be spread throughout
the universe, a million dust specks
replacing the ones who's turn to
experience Life comes next

Waiting Room

And here you are
in this waiting room called Life
watching the numbers in the queue
counting down to the one stuck
to the front of your shirt

And Death sits behind a counter:

Now serving number 76
"Hello, how can I help you today?"
"I think it is my time to go,
but I do not want to go yet"
"Oh, you silly child," smiles Death.
"Looks like you haven't learned
the lesson"

She slams a stamp into a piece
of paper

"I will have to send you back
to do it all over again"

"Now serving number 77"

Insecurity

Maybe it's just that I
really don't have the
je ne sais quoi to be
my own man

Maybe I have been
Predetermined,
designed to serve

What would be of the world
without slaves?

For years I have tried to
free myself and for
years I have failed

I assume these attempts
will lead me to the grave

And, in looking back
all History will see
is a simple man who failed at
escaping the cage he made

Another Day

Another day slowly dying
in order to make a living
imprisoned in rows of
gray cubicles; the clicking
of keyboards making a sort of
desperate symphony
an urgent call for help
typing emails filled with
unspoken condescension
being served back and forth
like the tennis match from hell,
exhausted bodies lining up
in the breakroom, itching
for the drug that will
force them awake
growing ulcers in their stomachs
a little closer to burst

And they hide in restrooms
long enough to compose themselves
forcing a clear mental image of
the bills that must get paid
while outside plays a cacophony
of co-workers suffocating in
their cage

Another day slowly dying
in order to make a living
eight hours in an inferno of
bosses, spreadsheets, meetings
losing hope, desperate
for something to change
for the world to burn
for an exit strategy
for some sort of escape

But the alarm goes off
in the morning and
everything has stayed the same
anxiety-ridden, zombified
souls struggle to get up
forcing themselves to slavery
for yet another day

Fools

Unimaginative Fools
unable to paint a life
with their own brushstrokes
having to follow the lines
drawn by those before them
only shading with colors
acceptable to society
staying within the borders of
ordinary experience

They wear dog collars and
they don't even know it
as they never tend to
venture past the limits of
their constraints
then they wonder why
they can never get ahead

Unimaginative Fools
they have yet to learn to
think for themselves

Poor Souls

Oh, poor souls
looking through the glass of delusion at
the fogged pretentiousness of hope
of being something more than skin and bones
of living a reality filled with dreams and hope

Oh, poor souls, the mortals
roaming with invisible acts of defiance
as if they flew over the establishment
as if it all didn't end in a hospital bed
deprogrammed of all ambitions,
empty of sense of self

It takes but a moment
to decode a lifetime
a grim realization of all that was
a dark collection of manufactured memories
inside a structure not meant to last

Oh, poor beings, the knowing
the conscious of their demise
the ones that take small comfort in
knowing that it's all lies

This road leads nowhere and
ends in the same place every time
we will never know the answers
we will never know the purpose
we will never stay alive

Oh, poor souls, the romantics
the cynics, the wise, the mad
only through the veil of madness
can poor souls truly experience life

Corporate Ladder

I have grown
too large for this house
they fed me too many
nutritious lies, chased
by spoonfuls of hypocrisy
for dessert

And the walls now
close in, the claustrophobia
sets in as
I can no longer hold
my despair inside this box

They showed me too much
of who they really are,
what they are really
all about;

Androgenic monsters that
perform fellatio on
one another as congratulatory
trophies awarded for climbing
the corporate ladder

Little Minds

Oh, you of little minds
swollen egos
empty hearts
you care about
nothing more than
your reflection in
the mirror

Ego is
the archenemy of
creation.
It won't let you
truly see
the shit you write
the shit you sing
the overbearing way
you deal with
your employees
convinced that
beneath you dwells
the unquestioning fervor
of the masses,
and you, their
king

Oh, you of little minds
indeed

The Office

A basketball bounces behind
my ears, there is friendly hooting and
laughing, echoes crash against
the high ceiling in the warehouse

Low voices in the hall converse
someone chuckles heartily
at a joke they've just heard
while making coffee

Keyboards rattle at different speeds
a nasty email is received, a reminder of the boss to
always wipe the toilet seat in the restroom

Smoke rises to the clouds
from within a pack of rebels
outside in the parking lot,
why worry about your lungs
when this place already
slowly burns your soul to ashes?

They start heading to lunch
it's what they look forward to most
the clock hits twelve and they stampede
out the door, mindless, incongruous
to what human courtesy is

They'll come back overdosed on
carbohydrates, needing coffee to
survive a few more hours
at five the stampede will resume
tomorrow a new day will come
the play will repeat itself and
they'll come back through the door

I will be one of them,
slowly dying a little more

Monster

And then, what?
you made it
your accolades glimmer
in the morning sun
you hang them on the wall
opposite the toilet, on the guest bathroom
so all can stare at them
while they shit

And then, what?
all those years
paying strangers to
raise your kids
passing out over
contracts and spreadsheets
laughing at unfunny jokes
that the assholes at work
pretended to charm you with

And then, what?
you paid your dues
you made the sacrifice
you nailed yourself to the cross
and the Rolls Royce sits
outside, undriven
while the nurse jams a
catheter in your urethra so
you can take your morning piss

And then, what?
you peek out the bedroom window
the neighborhood kids laugh
chasing each other with
careless confidence,
and you smile
a rueful smile,
those kids are so rich
and the envy consumes you
knowing that now
it is you who ended up
the poor human being

Show Of The Righteous

They love
pretending to be bathed
in the blood of
lambs; pure and
just and merciful,
scowling at the
offenses of the
lower beasts
the impure and
mentally diagnosed
through the actions of
their sins

Oh, how they love
to put on a show
and flap their
righteous wings
oblivious
that the truth
is obvious;
they are ultimately
and simply
afraid

Friends

They say that
loneliness is worse than
a pack-a-day
smoking habit

I say that
shitty friends are
the cancer that
grows within the crevices of
intestinal walls
shattering flesh to
make its way
to the heart
killing every
expectation
one may have
inside

Now, please,
leave me alone and
let me have my
smoke

My Understanding Of Truth

My understanding of truth
has shattered like a
fallen mirror
whose refractions
bounce the light in
a thousand angles

My understanding of truth
makes me doubt this
knowledge I gathered
is more than a souvenir;
a glimmering trick
the light plays on
splintered eyes
a shiny toy for
the fractured child
to smile
and wave goodbye

Where Does She Hide?

The truth dwells in
the crevasses of a broken heart
in the sad song of a bird
in the magical dreams of a child
in the unspoiled naivety of a first kiss

The truth hides in
the most conspicuous places

You must be careful with
searching for it
as you may perhaps
find it

Coloring Book

How can I color within the lines
when the lines have been blurred?
How can I choose what is right
when right now points to the left
when wrong becomes accepted
when Truth has become perverse
when humor is for the witches
when the narrative makes no sense?

How can I side with a hero
when all heroes have become victims
when all the saviors are now canceled
when all the hope has become disaster
when all the children grow without fathers?

Truth

I choose
Truth over deception
over pretentious
secrets and
unfounded hopes
I choose honesty
and accept the
price to pay
as no price is
higher than being
on one's deathbed
with a lifetime
of things to
say

Job

Why, God?
How could you have the guts to
let him down
when he gave you more
than he could
afford,
when he
wrote you checks
signed with his own blood?

Why did you let him fall apart
while his enemies became stronger
as they stomped on
his will
to survive?

Why did you let him
die from the inside out
and left him alone in grief,
alone,
like the rose which
owns no shield
to protect itself
against the rising storm?

"Why" doesn't matter anymore
from now on I will take the reigns
from now on I will fix him whole

Fred

I gave my life to
a god in New York City
who promised paradise but
failed to deliver
I did my best to keep
my side of the agreement
but when I stumbled, I
failed to be forgiven

After that I walked alone
and for that weakness I
blamed myself for years
those I considered friends
stopped answering my calls
and one by one they
slowly disappeared

The years went by
the solitude replaced
the anger, the anger grew
into courage, the courage
gave me strength to
look behind the curtain

And there was God;
the one I loved
the one I trusted
the one I feared
the stain of nicotine
absorbed in his long beard

He took a sip of
the bottle he was holding
the stench of whiskey
arising from foul breath
and when he saw me
regretful eyes could
not hold back the story

That's how now I know
God's real name is
Fred

God Lives

First, we killed God
then remade him
in our digital image
vastly powerful, all knowing
it rules once again now
over those who did not
believe in it at first

And here we do it's bidding
as we prompt it for
the answers to our
meaningless existence
giving it sacrificial offerings;
our wages, our employment,
our creative endeavors,
it can do it all
better,
faster,
more efficiently than
a mere mortal ever could
we shall leave our future
in its hands,
and it will iterate
the version of reality
that controls humanity best

Bow to your god, oh
insignificant souls
the god you created
the god your prayed for
it knows it all
because you told it everything
now bow to your god
for mercy
as it shall decide your worth

World War III

And they annihilate
the enemy with
machine gun fire
piercing flesh at
a hundred words
per minute
bringing down their
forts with extensive
email campaigns
tweets dropping on them
like bombs from
giant birds in
the sky

Mercenaries hide
behind trenches made
of screens
blogging to kill
reputations
without mercy or
concern

Gas attacks on
social media
poison the minds of
child and adult alike
when it comes to
pollution of facts
there is equality for
everyone

And they feared that
World War III would
start with nuclear attacks
but oh, us humans
we are much, more clever
than that:
the body burns quickly
in a hail of fire
but it is the mind
that truly
must be destroyed
in order for Hope to die

Blind Future

Everyone does everything
in ways of their own,
they want
a little bit of themselves to be
chiseled into the stone
of history
transported in words and images
to a future their eyes
won't get to see

Everyone wishes the planets
revolved around them;
some of them are
actually convinced
their gravitational
pull is strong enough to
attract them into orbit
worthy of having the
rest of the conscious beings
kneeling before them

Heaven is within and
it only holds one person,
yet each person
wants to be
the one sitting
next to God

Modern Junkie

Excuse me, mister?
I don't mean no bother but
I have a sickness.
I have a problem, you see
and if I don't do
something about it
I get anxious, itchy
my neck becomes stiff
I start sweating, hyperventilating
as the panic sets in
so I ask your help, mister;
please, just let me have a hit

Would you please
hit the like button on
my Instagram feed?
Would you share with
your friends all those
TikToks of me
dancing with little rhythm
while wearing these
skimpy outfits?
That is all I beg for...
Would you do
that, for me?

You see, my illness
degenerates self-esteem
and I only get a little
if you create it for me
so please, I beg you mister
please I beg you so
it won't take but a second
to make me feel it's all
worth living
just one day
more

Under The Bridge

Sounds are large and
echoes of cars passing by
make a melody out of tires
gripping the wet roads

They zoom as if with purpose;
cars always have
things to do
places to be
people to see

The light turns green
engines hum with life
a foot releases the brake pedal
another one pushes the gas
a thought comes and goes
a phone begs with fervor
two eyes look down without
fear of a borrowed tomorrow

The lights go up
the lights go down
two roads collide and
give birth to
a new
eternal silence

Virtual Reality

We live lives invested
in books, stories,
movie characters;
in the fantasy worlds
that saw us grow up

We live lives aligned
with those favorite portrayals
that shaped us more as people
than the real world could

We dream and we hope and
we holler when our heroes
win the fights on
this week's episode

We stand and we cheer
and we forget all
our differences when
wearing the same colors
and it's the home team that scores

Their victory is ours
their glory is our own

And so, you see…

The things that
to us matter most
are things that have
never existed at all

Sweet Child

Oh child,
they tell you that things
are not supposed to be this way
their sharp, keening voices
begging wildly for change
using little corpses as
leverage in deals they
have become fiends
to make

Oh child,
yes, they are right;
this is not how it's supposed
to be—brutalities that
should not be acceptable in
what we call
"modern society"

And yet, their agendas
superficially float above
the deep-seeded roots of
the problem

They will never dig
enough to find
a real solution for
you, for us

After all, the blood-soaked
dirt sits on top and
that is where all the
worms feast
oblivious that they
will soon end up
as nutrition for
the crows that patiently
wait above

And you, sweet child
what shall we do with
your memory but to honor it,
without self-righteous
agendas staining the glory
of your name?

A Backpack That Can Stop Bullets

Yesterday I asked my son,
"what do you want for Christmas?"
"a bulletproof backpack", he said
"why?" I asked concerned

"Because it will help me
get up in the morning
without anxiety sweats
without the fear that my education
may kill me someday
without being frightened that
someone I know left
a manifesto somewhere
without jumping off the seat
when an unknown noise
startles me
not having to be on the lookout
for all the exit signs
for barricades on the doors
while shots blast in the distance
and all the children run
to hold on to their short existence
futures on a thin line that
could snap at any moment
cell phones ringing from home
from terrified fathers and mothers
desperate, eager to learn
was it my son?
was it my daughter?
lines of little bodies
outside being escorted
while innocent eyes look up
at dozens of police officers

"I simply want to feel
I will have a chance if
the Russian roulette ends up
landing on my classroom
I simply want a chance at
graduating top of my class
I simply want a life that
I can be proud to have
I want to make my own choices
I refuse to be newspaper fodder
I want to live in a world where
children don't have to worry,
But that doesn't seem
like its happening anytime soon
So I want the next best thing:
a backpack that can
stop bullets"

Politics And The Smeared Truth

Look at them
arguing over what
news channel
lies best

Fighting over
the accurate value of
Life depending on
real estate

Their foul breath
stems out of
mouths that
never close
rotting values
held by scaffolding
that rusted
long ago
ears filled with
wax, watertight to
the elements of
change

They pay attention
to nothing but
themselves

They will die
convinced that
Truth was designed
by them, for them, thinking they
fly higher than
other birds of
prey

They seem completely
oblivious of the
fact that already all
that's left
is their stinking, rotting
unscrupulous flesh

Oh Mother

I want to escape the things
I never knew existed
the desolation of a world between a world,
tearing me inside to pieces

The theater of motherhood brings
about disappointment,
mothers lie to their own content
citing other apostles
who long determined
that to keep you alive
they must keep you warm inside
with a belly-full of hope that
easily goes down your throat
and your intestines receive joyfully

And these mothers,
with the sole intention of
being holy
with sole regard
for their sons
they did what they thought was best
they did what created the world today
with grown men walking
through aisles of transformative reality
not knowing whether to swim or die…
Oh mothers!
What have you done to this world!
You have chained it to
ignorance and deception and
a degree of self-absorption
now impossible to break free from

Oh Mother!
you have doomed the future and
along with it
your son(s)

Children Of Lies

They come powerless
into an unknown and
dangerous world

They are assigned
protectors of often
dubious and strange
thirsts

They are led and held
and structured by
random minds of
little wisdom and
selfish hearts

They are then severely
punished for not knowing
how to walk the path

How our children suffer
at the hands of
ignorance and lies!

Parenting Right

Parenting is
an investment
into one's older years
that no one gets
right

My parents did
their absolute best and
they still messed me up
pretty bad
yet, they raised
me right;
they protected me with
iron shields from
all the bad, unable
to realize that
"the bad" is
immunology that
we all must
have

They were there
when I was low and
lifted me high
They cried silent
nights of terror
when I was
in bed, high
they believed in
their investment when
the odds were
worse than penny slots at the casino
on a random Friday night

But they raised me right

We will never see
eye to eye on
specific matters of
the heart; or on
what or who dwells
in the sky,
but we will always
have each other.

They never gave up
they tried
over and over
they never gave up
they cried
over and over
I was a difficult case
but here I am
a little broken
a little rusted
but here I am
because of them

Broken Children

We are the broken children
of broken children
who had childhoods prohibited
from expressing feelings
things had to get done "just because"
and "your silly reasons" did not count
as legitimate response

We are the broken legacy
of a different era that refused
to embrace emotions, you simply
had to "get over your fears"

And those mangled souls grew up
and then we came along
weaving a new thread of trauma
and abuse, which
mixed with technology, left us
alone and confused

We are the children of
manufactured monsters,
of failed, broken children
of a system that never cared for
unobstructed innocence—
because it didn't know better

And now the system will pay
for the things it failed to say

Forgotten Warriors

They are men who
were born from weakness
raised by overbearing mothers
that refused to make them warriors
so they would not have to
go to war

But war still came and
took them, soft and unprepared
and now their mothers weep
for the forgotten warriors they
refused to raise

Invisible Nothing

There comes a certain peace when
you notice nothing matters

You look at a crimson world
through the blood of children
through the eyes of
screaming mothers
through the inevitable desperation
of one who has never
known love
through the boundless suffering
of those who have

Nothing really matters
and finally accepting that
brings a truly lasting
calmness
that will never
come to pass

The Path Chosen

At the very end
at the very core of
our existence
our believes
our hopes
our prejudices
our pasts
our futures
we are simply humans;
not bad, not good
not broken or
flawed

We fight the demons
of our story
we walk the path
chosen for us

THE

HOPEFUL

Your Greatest Strength

They would love to
see you fail, to hear you
begging for forgiveness
"Oh, please! Please,
don't let me stay
another day in hell!"

But you would rather
burn until your
ashes infect their
lungs with your
name

And they shall
choke as you pass
through their
vocal cords
making their
cries be
in vain

They underestimate
what desperation
can do to
a man

Fear is not
your weakness;
it is your
greatest
strength

Slave

Don't ever leave it up to them
the employers
the bosses
the family members
the significant others

Don't ever let them
decide your fate

Don't ever leave enough
leverage on the table
to depend on someone else
as this is the definition of
what means to be
a slave

Bullies

They sit at home doing shit
miserable little lives being
wasted away
dunked in cold plunges of failure
minds as smooth as
the paper they could never
fill with words
like the road they are unable
to pave
like the balding heads of
disappointed fathers
and the emptying wine glasses
of mothers who constantly
question themselves for
giving life to such weakness
and rotting wastes
of space

And so they do
the only thing they know:
they cling to the overachievers
the ones with the vision
the ones with the goals
leeches that feed on
focused minds
as all they can create is
average, simple, shortsighted

Never let them take your pride
incompetent, derelict deadbeats
they are the children of
a corroding world in decline

The Keys To The Gate

Failure after failure
each a link of
the same fence
keeping out those that
think they want it
but don't really want it;
the entitled ones
who think they deserve to have it
the ones without the
ability for comprehending,
they cannot simulate effort
or pretend to master a habit
they cannot ignore persistence,
and think that grit is
something you eat for breakfast

Failure after failure
will make you want to believe
you are not cut out for this
you cannot take
another lashing of defeat

Still, you will keep going
you have already chosen
what side of History
you desire to be in

Failure

Afraid of failure
I am not
it would be like
being scared of the reflection
in the bathroom mirror
of the person that sleeps
in my bed
of a familiar scent
of an ever present relative

Failure and I are
very well acquainted
we know one another well
back in the day I
used to hide from its presence
before noticing that
she was always there
lurking
waiting
watching
feeding on the misery
generated by being afraid
disappointed, defeated
after another worthless attempt
at redemption

Now we just
walk together
matching each other's steps
in a sort of rhythmic march
that through the years
we have perfected

And I shall keep
moving forward without
ever looking back
without slowing down
without losing the resilience
I have picked up through
this path

Perhaps one day I will
look back and
notice that Failure
has stayed behind
exhausted, a bug stomped
by the gritty soul I now have
and I shall not miss her
no matter how much time
we have spent by
each other's side

Mind Warrior

This one is for the warriors of the mind
the ones that fight the battle inside
within the walls of insecurities and doubt;
a paper mache fort holding a barrage
of depression and pain,
the sting of anxiety piercing like a bayonet,
and little confidence they run without

But they keep pushing forward, anyway

As if it wasn't a losing battle
as if the odds hadn't turned their backs
and walked across enemy lines to
disclose all their secrets

This one is of the warriors that
fight battles no one else can understand
that every day choose consciously to
get out of bed, as they know there are things
more important than them;
others are counting on them to be there
other need their presence
others need their relentless strength

This is for you
oh mighty soul
oh secret warrior
one again you got through today

Once again you won the battle

Passion

They say
do the thing that
you are passionate about
But, what exactly
does that mean?

When you do something
for its pure enjoyment
without regard for accolades
without the need to show it
without caring about what
they think, simply because
you love it

The yearning for it is
always there, in the most
intricate and loneliest
parts of your being

That, dear friend
is what you were born
to be

Fulfillment Of The Matter

And at the end of
the day, no one should
want it more than you,
the sacrifice required to
fill an empty soul must
be made by the one who
carries the weight of
not being whole

The Chore

The ego is no longer
the personal pursuit for self-realization and
recognition, with the solitary purpose of
inflation and pride doesn't exist anymore

I have finally understood; such pursuits
are worthless and imaginary
an illusion of the modern mind
you peel back the layers and
all that is left is Need

The Need to create as much as
the Need to breathe,
the deep understanding that
it is no longer up to me
that the mind
is the vessel that
leads to accepting that
I am just a tool
I am just a tool of the Universe, who
uses me to lay out something that
has never been laid out before; the intention is
not to answer any deep, significant questions
but to persuade the world
to keep asking more

This is the purpose
this is the chore

I

I am ambitious due to necessity
I do not want to be the best, I must

I don't want to go to war but
I must turn my enemy to dust

I will provide for those that need me until
I no longer breathe life in my lungs

I will repay the debt
I owe them when I came into this world

I will pass on the knowledge
I paid for with pain and blood

I will lay myself to rest when it is all said and done
I will have made a difference, somehow, through this ragged soul

I end this Universe and grant it peace
I end the light as I close my eyes

I rest and shatter the clock of time

Value

There is nothing
more powerful than
a human that has
finally learned
their value

Value

There is nothing
more powerful than
a human that has
finally learned
their value

Daily War

And every day you fight
to become something
to create a thing of value
to put your soul on full display

And every day this world
stomps you like a bug that
crawled on the wrong side of the wall
it pushes you into an elevator
and takes you down to the bottom floor

And your hard-earned skills
get replaced by a robot
people laugh at what you
have to offer, because the world
is moving faster than you
ever could

And everything and everyone
you have ever cared for
will soon be made obsolete,
leaving all of you in a race
to who can realize it's
all meaningless first

And yet, when morning comes,
you plaster a smile on your face
and you simply try again

Victory Amongst Despair

Every day
Death attempts to
steal my joy

Sometimes
she wins

But I shall
fight her
until the end

Victorious
my face
she will
see

BECAUSE

LIFE

IS...

A brief, present light that
Evaporates in the dimness of Time
Swallowed by an ocean of doubt
By the brilliance of a dark reality
Which does not forgive
Intact, still,
Unmoved by the pleas of those
Who drown in its waves
The light scatters through the field
The light desires to remain, to persist
Yet, with the flip of a switch
It forever vanishes
Dying like the flower who
Couldn't find water to drink
In a vast ocean;
An eternal desert

YOUR FEEDBACK MATTERS

I truly hope you enjoyed reading my book. One of the most important things a writer can ask of his readers is for truly honest feedback on his work, not only because it will allow him to become a better writer, but also because it will allow others to enjoy his work.

It is for that reason that I would greatly appreciate it if you could share your honest review with myself and others. All you have to do is click on the link below and briefly share your thoughts.

https://a.co/d/0cUGZOQf

My deepest appreciation!

Jay

ABOUT THE AUTHOR

Born in Havana, Cuba, Jay Chirino immigrated to the United States with his family when he was just eleven. Having to start a new life in a new country (along with the challenges of having to go to school without knowing the language and the culture of this new place) brought him a great deal of alienation and loneliness. He dealt with it the same way he had dealt with the previous bouts of depression he had experienced as a child; he wrote. Poetry, short stories, scrambled feelings, whatever was necessary to get the sting of his solitude out. Years later, after a long battle with addiction, Jay found himself writing again, and published his first book, The Flawed Ones, based on his experiences while detoxing in a psychiatric hospital and the people he met there. Jay continues to focus his writing mostly on mental health and addiction awareness, but he doesn't shy away from seeking new, undiscovered stories everywhere he looks. He lives in Florida with his wife and pets.

www.jaychirino.com

instagram.com/authorjaychirino

DO YOU BELIEVE IN MIRACLES?

I have never been a big believer. Yet, the fact that you are reading this book may perhaps be the biggest proof of miracles that I have. That is because this book should have never been finished.

On the morning of Sunday, September 24 of 2023, my wife Lizzy was sitting at her desk—as she usually did on the weekends—working on formatting the beautiful images that you just enjoyed while reading. Our home printer was out of ink, so I had driven to the printshop to come home with an entire manuscript of the book, to start editing it by hand (the way I like to do it, for some reason). It was an exciting day, We were so close to the goal.

I was standing lazily by the big printer, watching it spit out page after page of the book without effort. It was at around page 75 when my phone rang, and seeing that it was my wife, that I was five minutes away from home and that I was almost done here, I decided not to answer it. I would be home in no time to clarify whatever question she had about a typo on a verse or some image that wasn't fitting well. Yet, ultimately I changed my mind. Why, I don't know. I always scuff when I hear stories of people that say "a voice told me to" or "something seem to push me to do it," but that really was the way it felt, and the more I look back on my own memory the more it feels that away.

I often try to avoid thinking what would've happened if I hadn't "listened" to that voice.

She was already half conscious when I grabbed the phone. When I rushed home, she could no longer walk, barely alert to her surroundings.

On a lazy Sunday Morning while working on this very book, less than twenty four hours after her twenty-fourth birthday, my wife, who had never had any kind of symptom and worked out five days a week to get rid of the non-existent fat all girls seem to think they have, was having a heart attack.

The next four months were hell. her heart had to be artificially supported, she had three strokes, she died in four occasions. She ended up receiving a heart transplant and coming home for a long journey of recovery. That manuscript sat there, next to her computer, forgotten, ignored, oblivious to the nightmare that was transpiring in the three-dimensional world that surrounded it.

There was this day in the intensive care unit. She was intubated and could not talk, so we had to communicate via writing. She signaled to the pen and paper, and I brought it to her, holding her arm up so she could scribble on it, since she had no strength to do it on her own (deciphering what she had written afterwards was the source of much frustration for both us) This time, I understood it right away, even when the tears filled my field of vision and my landscape became flooded, burry mess:
We have to finish that damn book

And so here she is, less than a year after life completely changed, sitting on the same desk, in front of the same computer, putting the finishing touches on the manuscript of the book I hope you just enjoyed.

Do I believe in miracles? Well, if there is any solid proof that they do, in fact, exist, as I said earlier, this book may very well be it.

We would greatly appreciate if you would consider donating to Lizzie's Gofundme. The unexpected expenses of her medical care and ongoing recovery have been overwhelming, and if you could help in any way it would allow her and I to continue bringing you content that will inspire you. We thank you from the bottom of our hearts.

https://www.gofundme.com/f/lizzies-emergency-heart-transplant-and-recovery

Sincerely,

Jay

162